Powerful, fears surface ... not denied, but growing hope and expectancy are there as well. Mary has captured the emotions surrounding the loss of a loved one in a way that not only honors her Dale but brings hope to others as well.

> —*Dr. Ken Isom*, Associate Pastor,
> The Bridge AG, Mustang, Oklahoma

As I read these heart-born poems by Mary Roberts, my first thought was, *This is going to help so many people so much.* Every person who reads this book who has suffered loss (and that would be all of us), will quickly identify with Mary's pain and find in her poems a cathartic healing.

Dale Roberts was my first cousin. I got to know him (and Mary) much better in the last few years. These poems are a gift to all of us. Dale and Mary were literally meant for each other. They had a deep, abiding love. Of course, that makes the pain more intense ... and the memories more precious.

Recently I have lost a dear friend and colleague (whose name, interestingly, was Dale). These poems have taken on even deeper meaning for me. I know they will strengthen you as well.

—*Dr. David Shibley*, President,
Global Advance

Mary Roberts' enormous literary skills have been lying dormant, just waiting for a shove to catapult her into action. The emotional and physical impact of the death of her loving husband Dale has done just that. Her poignant *death* poems grip the heart and soul, ultimately allowing the grief to pour out and slowly dissipate.

—*Linda Cole*, Teacher,
Sayre Schools, Sayre, Oklahoma

Mary puts her emotions out there as therapy for us all. Enjoy her poetry as she takes us with her on her journey through great love, great sorrow, and great faith.

—*Connie Harris*, Co-Owner,
An Affair of the Heart,
Oklahoma City, Oklahoma

I thought Mary Roberts' poems were so poignant. She is so honest and loving in her words. Thank you, Mary, for sharing them with us. I feel privileged to have heard her heart during such a time of loss. I know they will be healing and comforting to many.

—*Naomi Shibley*, Global Advance

What Do I Do Now?

What Do I Do Now?

Poems for Those Left Behind

Mary Cole Roberts

TATE PUBLISHING & Enterprises

Published by Tate Publishing & Enterprises, LLC
127 E. Trade Center Terrace | Mustang, Oklahoma 73064 USA
1.888.361.9473 | www.tatepublishing.com

Tate Publishing is committed to excellence in the publishing industry. The company reflects the philosophy established by the founders, based on Psalm 68:11,
"The Lord gave the word and great was the company of those who published it."

Book design copyright © 2009 by Tate Publishing, LLC. All rights reserved.
Cover design by Amber Gulilat
Interior design by Stefanie Rooney
Author Photo by Loretta Cribbs

Published in the United States of America

ISBN: 978-1-60696-954-0
1. Poetry, Inspirational & Religious
2. Self-Help, Bereavement
09.04.30

Dedication

To Dale, my husband and best friend, who served as the inspiration for these poems, and to my Lord and Savior, from whom the words came.

Acknowledgements

To my parents, Bert and Willie Cole, who gave me life and taught me girls were just as important as boys; my sister-in-law, Linda Cole, who first encouraged me to do this; Janie Russell, who has kept me sane during these first months; Connie Harris, who read the first dozen poems and told me to go for it; Brother Ken Isom, who has been a constant spiritual blessing; Joshua Price, to whom I read *Lord How Do I Know?* and told him it wasn't finished, to which he replied, "Sounds finished to me!" Also, to my many friends and family who offered encouragement along the way, and last but not least, Dr. Matt Crespo, who knows the true meaning of *the* healing physician.

Special thanks to Tate Publishing, and to those who made this dream a fine tuned reality through their editing, layout, and design skills: Ryan Bell, Angela Faulkner, Amber Gulilat, and Stefanie Rooney.

Table of Contents

Foreword

The loss of a loved one by death causes feelings of loss, anger, frustration, and sorrow. How can someone else express in words, beautifully delivered in poetry, some of the exact same feelings and experiences that I went through in the loss of my husband of fifty-one years? Mary Roberts does just that! She expresses the shock of knowing your spouse is gone even though you should have expected his death. She shares the frustration of all the business affairs that have to be dealt with when you can't even cope with your grief. She touches on the anger you feel with your loved one for leaving you with all the work that were *his jobs* to do. She shares the agony of the empty house and the lonely bed. She writes two-sided conversations with her husband, sharing doubts of her ability to go on, but recognizing his unfailing faith in her ability to do just that even though he is gone. She cries out to God, challenging his decision but submitting to his will.

Have you yet experienced this gamut of emotional stress? I have! Thank you, Mary for helping me and encouraging all of us who have lost our dear ones to know that there is someone else who has suffered as we have, but there is also someone who will go through this dark valley with us; he cries as we cry, but he whispers as he holds our hand, "I will never leave you; trust in me; I know what is best!"

Melva W. Curtis, EdD
Professor Emeritus,
Mid-America Christian University

Preface

When you get start reading this book of poetry, I hope you can say, "How does she *know* what I am feeling?" If the truth be told, I don't know what you are feeling in the loss of your loved one, but I definitely do know what I am feeling in the loss of mine.

I have always written words of comfort or encouragement or even chastisement for friends and relatives whom I felt were in need of them. They have always been gratefully received, even those of reprimand. The words have always been meant to assist or help.

But this was different. My precious husband's death hit too close to home, touched my very soul, and ripped my heart in half. There are a few love poems at the end that were obviously written in much happier times and one poem that relates to my momma's oh so recent death. The rest of the poems were written when I was sitting in my husband's hospital room, holding his hand on the last day of his life or in the weeks and months following his death when I couldn't sleep or otherwise function. I think they will all touch your heart.

In times past, when the words came to me in the dark of night and very early morning, I sometimes chose to sleep, instead of getting up and writing the words down. The next time I tried to capture them, they were gone. I now know to stop whatever I am doing and write down the words the Lord gives me. As you can tell, I do believe the message comes from God; I only serve as the messenger.

After the funeral, several friends and relatives encouraged me to submit the poetry for publication. I held my breath, hit send, and you know the rest of the story.

You will see for yourself *What Do I Do Now?* comes directly from the heart. I hope these poems give you the same measure of comfort and relief it gave me to write them. God bless you during this difficult time.

Mary Cole Roberts

Introduction

Dale and I met at the Oklahoma City Festival of the Arts in 1980, where we were both working as volunteers. The third day of the festival, I was leaving with my parents for my brother Brian's wedding, and I asked him to walk me to my car. Anyone who knew me then will tell you I didn't *need* anyone to walk me to my car—this was during my "women's lib" stage of life.

On Friday, December nineteenth, he asked me to marry him. We wanted to get married shortly after the first of the year, but scheduling conflicts weren't going to allow our nuptials until April. We didn't want to wait that long, so we decided to get married on Monday, the twenty-second. The day before the wedding, I could tell something was bothering him.

Finally, late in the afternoon, he asked, "Would you mind terribly if we didn't get married tomorrow?"

I took a deep breath and replied, "No, if you don't mind telling me why not!"

"It is my old wedding anniversary."

Tuesday, the twenty-third, we paid fifty cents to park at the Oklahoma County Courthouse. A judge on his way to court performed the ceremony in an alcove somewhere in the building. To this date, I can't tell you his name.

We went to the Oklahoma Tourism and Recreation (OTR) office where I worked to tell the boss and everyone else about our marriage.

I was the Travel Development Coordinator at OTR, so I was out of town a lot the first several years we were married. Part of my job was to work with travel professionals within the United States, showing them the glories of Oklahoma and why their clients should come here, rather than go for vacation somewhere else in the US. Sometimes Dale could join me on the weekends at his own expense; then the woman who did international travel quit. Her job became mine as well. Travel-wise, that would have put me in town less than six weeks for six months. We were newlyweds, so I quit.

I now had a lot of extra time. This meant you could have eaten off any floor, anywhere in the house during my first six months at home—it was that clean.

Crafts of all types were something I already did,

but Dale encouraged me to find additional interests; so I took up gardening, cake and candy making, and, later, machine embroidery, and quilting.

Growing up, both of us always raised vegetable gardens. We soon discovered our methods of crop raising to be totally different. We worked through our differences together. Then we took a beginning horticulture class. I wanted to plant everlastings—they were not available; neither were the hot peppers we wanted. We raised them from seed instead. Dale always helped me plant all these little babies in the ground. In a typical summer, we planted fifty to sixty flats of flowers, several hundred caladiums, and hot peppers of all types. Both of us really enjoyed spicy hot salsa, but store brands contained too much salt; we developed our own recipe.

I saw no reason why Dale should have to work all week and do yard chores on the weekend, so I took over yard duties with an electric-start Honda lawnmower. Of course, he still had to fix and repair everything. If it didn't start when I tried to turn it on, I was through!

We always thought throwing away grass clippings in the trash was a waste, but putting them under the vegetables brought more grass, so I "designed" a compost pile. Dale refined it; we built it. Mulching helps retain moisture and cut down on watering a bit—a necessity in the Oklahoma heat. Dale found an electric chipper shredder for me. His cohorts at work thought he was nuts the year he bought caladium bulbs for Valentine's Day as my present. I was ecstatic. Our redwood deck needed replacing, so we did it. Dale taught me how to use a drill driver. Adding Bradford pear trees to our front yard created a shade bed, so we put in a bench and a winding sidewalk.

Dale was a true computer geek; designing programming originally on a Radio Shack computer—that was total Greek to me. It was binary (I think that is what you call it, anyway). Even after the computer became user-friendly, I resisted. I am not much for change, you see, and going from hand-written or typed to writing and viewing on a computer screen was definitely a change. Then I discovered the world of email, ordering on line, and keeping records of my writings.

We began attending The Bridge AG (Assembly of God) in Mustang. Among several mission projects was a yearly trip to one of the Indian reservations in Arizona where the men build a church from the slab up. The women cook and teach Vacation Bible School. We signed on. Dale learned carpentry from his father, who was a finish carpenter, so he built a fancy balance beam called Buddy Barrel, an AG character who generates a contest between the boys and girls to see who can raise the most money in coins. Buddy Barrel "holds" a metal bucket on each arm. The weight of the coins tips the balance one way (girls) or the other (boys). Buddy Barrel was beautiful and worked perfectly. In 2006, the San Carlos AG gave over one thousand dollars, through Buddy Barrel, to missions. Shortly before Dale retired, I got interested in quilting, largely due to the influence of my momma and both grandmothers. My momma machine-pieced a quilt, then sent it to the local quilter to finish; my grandmothers pieced the quilt top, then hand-quilted it to the backing or also sent it to the local quilter. I wanted to do the final part only—quilt the quilt top (front), backing (back), and batting (middle) together. This piece of equipment was going to be a major financial investment, so for vacation in 2003, Dale and I went to the International Quilt Festival in Houston where we bought a short arm quilting frame. If I had a problem with a pattern size for quilting, he fixed it. Quilting on a short arm was a bit of a challenge when you are quilting mostly queen and king size quilts;

after that, we bought a Gammill—the Mercedes of quilting machines. We rebuilt a room to hold this new tool. Dale began designing quilts. We wanted to take quality pictures of them, so he made an overhead railing on which to hang them. Many quilts, ours, as well as those of other quilters', have their "pictures" made there! We enjoyed this new endeavor together, never dreaming God had different plans for the two of us—plans he revealed to us in April of 2005.

Dale's prostate cancer reared its ugly head then. I told him he would never have to go to an appointment by himself. He only went to one alone. The first round was not that bad and the cancer was contained until January of 2007. More radiation later in 2007 (fall and winter) left him on narcotics and burn ointment.

How do I tell you about the radiation burns— the enormous area they covered on what was now a frail body? The quiet strength with which he bore them? How do I tell you about the drugs he initially refused to take, because they were narcotics, until the doctor gently, but firmly, patted him on the knee and told him to get over it; he was going to need them.

Or the smiles he always had for everyone,

even through the non-ceasing pain; the constant trips diarrhea caused after the constipation quit; the chemo port that refused to draw (maybe that should have told us something); the food he didn't want to eat because it didn't stay anywhere, but was painfully eliminated?

Or the February stay in the hospital, the trips to Wal-Mart or anywhere else that brightened his day, and the impatience I sometimes felt when I pushed the grocery cart and he slowly rolled his wheelchair behind me? *Oh, Dale, please forgive that impatience in me.* This was his only exercise.

How do I tell you about the joy we felt when family came to our home in May and he was able not only to go out to eat, but also to walk from the car into the restaurant with just the aid of a cane? Or the fold-up cot we bought so he could lie in the same room with me while I pieced the last quilt he ever saw me make?

Or the prayers we both prayed for this to pass? It did pass; but I am still here, and he is not.

I'd like to tell you about the peace and quiet reverence with which he read his Bible on the days he felt well and the devotionals his sister, Connie, shared with him.

I'd like you to know in my own words the wonderful man I knew and how life was being married to him. I want you to understand how he bore his suffering and pain in his final days on earth. I hope you can gently feel it. Dale was that kind of a man—gentle, full of life, fun, teasing, loving, and always concerned about others. He knew his God and had told a close friend he was not afraid of dying. He just thought he was going to make it home this time. He did make it home, home to his heavenly Father; just not the home where we both wanted him to return.

He was not just my husband. He was my best friend. There was only one Dale. I miss him every hour of every day. Now I face life without my husband at my side. Where do I go from here? I do not know. But I do know God is still with me—beside me. This is definitely not a road I chose; God chose it for me. Oh, God and Dale, help me walk this path alone.

How Do I?

How do I walk this path ... this path I go alone?

This is all so new to me ... I just want to go home.

My body flinches with every move ... my breathing is labored and fast.

My only question is, "How much longer are they going to make me last?"

I've led a good life up to now, fairly free of aches and pain.

If this breath is to be my last, let me take it without such physical strain.

God, I'm ready, I moan. Please take me home.

I'm ready ... I'm ready to see my new home.

I'm too weak to talk ... I can't stand on my own two feet.

I have no appetite ... all I want to do is sleep.

The drugs make me hallucinate ... how much more of this can I take?

Please answer me, Lord, is this to be my fate?

The medication doesn't begin to cover the agony.

Please, Lord, please! Will you please answer me?
My mind is scrambled; my pulse is weak.
I guess I'm ready ... my Savior to meet.
I cannot imagine this path alone.
I'm going home ...
Going home.

Mary Cole Roberts

How Do I Walk This Path?

*O*h, God, how do I walk this path?
This path I go alone.

How do I take these steps,
These steps now that he is gone.

Dale, where are you? I cannot see you! I can't feel you!
Where are you?

How do I go on?

My knees buckle.
My steps falter.

God, I cannot do this alone.

This is the path I have chosen for you, my child.
You can make it through.

Put one foot after the other;
I will take them with you.

He's here with me now, you know,
in his new home.

You will join him some day;
You, too, will come home.

This is a far better place than the world you know.
He has no more worries; only friends, no foes.

Your Dale is in no more physical pain.
He feels only joy, not strain.

Mary, you concentrate.
You CAN remember his face.

Just focus on the joys you've shared, the love you've both known.

He's here with me now. This IS his home.

What Do You Mean?

*A*nxious?
The word cannot begin to describe how I feel.

And you want me to pray for peace?
What?
Peace? There is no peace!

Not only peace, but the peace which passes all understanding...

Peace?

I am so tired. Can't I just go to sleep instead?

Trust?
What do you mean trust?

My husband is dying. I can see it happening with my own eyes.

Trust?
What do you mean the battle's not mine?

What do you mean!

It's God's? What?

What makes it God's battle?

Not mine?

Do not be anxious ... peace which passes all understanding ...

Cast all your anxiety upon him ... do not be anxious ... the peace of God, which transcends all understanding ... the battle is not yours ... Trust in the Lord ...

Oh. [1]

Lord, How Do I Know?

Lord, how do I know when I have reached the peace which passes all understanding?

How do I know when I get there?

Is anything any different?

Let me go. PLEASE!

The forced breathing ... the drug ridden haze ...
Sleeping nights. Sleeping days.

Turned left. Turned right.
Preventing bedsores.
Right!

Raising the head ... letting it down ...
Can't drink water ...
Only mush.

Can't get up ...
Way too weak.

Who's here?
Don't know ...
Fast asleep.

No food intake, only IVs ...

My God! My God! Help me PLEASE!

"I hurt!" I cry, as here in this bed I lie.

"I'm ready to die. I'm ready to die."

Mary Cole Roberts

No more feeding tube ... no more BiPap, PLEASE.
Let me go! Let me go!
PLEASE!

How Do I Find You?

$\mathcal{J}$ see you as you gag down those gigantic pills and hold you as they come up again.

Are you staying here for me? Don't do that please!

I don't want you to go; I will miss you terribly.
But, don't stay here for me.

I've heard heaven is a beautiful place. I don't know.
I haven't been there.

I do know that's where you will go when you leave.

I can't even imagine.
I do want to know.

How does it feel?
What's it like?
Where will you be?
How do I find you?

Mary Cole Roberts

I Am Ready to Say Goodbye

𝒟ear Dale,

I am ready to say goodbye,
although I do it with tear filled eyes.

Goodbye to you, the love of my life,
the one with whom I shared my most joyful moments.

Goodbye to you, the one who taught me patience;
who took me just as I was,
no questions asked.

Goodbye to you, Dale, the one who brought out the
very best in me;
who laughed when I laughed ... held me when I cried;

Who spoiled me and fulfilled my every wish,
who sang with me in the choir;

Who listened to me when I was hurt ...
or frustrated with the actions of others.

Whose humor was special;
who didn't mind explaining jokes
until I understood them.

Goodbye to you, Dale, a perfect husband
a gentle, thoughtful, loving man ...

Goodbye, Dale, you are the love of my life.

Goodbye.

Your wife, Mary XXOO

Oh, Dale

*O*h, Dale, I don't know what to say to you.
My grief is overwhelming.
And the quiet here in our home is truly quite
astounding.

These past few weeks we didn't really visit much.
There were no words left to say.

And though we both really knew it was the end,
I was not ready for you to go away.

I just wanted one more time to hear you say
"I love you and it's going to be okay."
But it isn't and you didn't, so that's the way
it has to be.

Your computer crashed—how weird is that?
Or was it really only a loose wire?
When into the safe I had to get
and moved all the files and boxes over to it.

I know you thoroughly enjoyed the ride
to the cemetery,
and felt compassion for us,
roasting in the heat of the limousine.

It was the way you would have taken
if you'd had the choice.
Back roads will never be the same for me.
I'll always hear your voice.

I long for your loving arms to me enfold and tell
me everything's all right.
Or to touch your face ...
or see your eyes.
But I have to be satisfied with pictures and memories now.

Oh, Dale! I don't know what to say, except

I truly love you.

Mary Cole Roberts

To the Captain
of the Ship

*T*o the Captain of the ship with whom I sailed uncharted seas.

If I'd known it would come to this, I'd have just stayed at home,

or at least have thrown away your keys.

The funeral's over; families gone. I can truly say I've never felt so all alone.

But it was also a blessing, to you have known.

I've understood from the start the possibility of death ...

but it always seemed so far away.

Now that it has come to pass, I see God must have sent you my way.

My heart is broken; my life changed;

I do not question going on.

But it all seems so strange to me now that you, too, are gone.

Each day you came with smile and grace my precious husband to see ...

and while his care you did undertake, you also
found time to minister to me.

The words you shared I won't forget, nor the Book
from which they came ...
and though time will erase
the memory of your face,
I shall never forget your name.

Those who know me best, laughed when I said ...
someone else was in charge.
They questioned how that came to pass,
their amusement quite large.

And as I take this path he chose for me,
I just wanted to say:

Thank you, from a Christian to a Christian,
for being a part of my husband's life
during his final days.

Is He the Angel You Have Sent?

Is he the angel you have sent me to help make the transition?
You knew I needed one.

Will this doctor's compassion and Christian care make this path easier to walk?

This path you have sent me down ...
alone ...
without Dale.

Should I have done something differently?
I have wondered frequently.

So what would it have been?
I don't know.

I couldn't have loved him any more than I already do.

I couldn't have cared for him any more than I did.

So what would it have been?

I honestly can't tell you.

How Do I Feel?

How do I write these words to say how I feel?
It's been over a month now and
I don't feel any different.

Where do I start this? Where do I begin?
How do I finish this? How do I fit in?

I miss you every day, every night, too.
The longer you are gone, the more I miss you.

I have no idea how I'm supposed to handle this,
no idea what was going through your mind.
I know you think I can handle this.
You must have been out of your mind.

I know there's a reason
for everything in God's plan,
but at the moment I certainly don't understand
any of this.

And all I want to know is why?
Why are you gone ...
and why am I still here?

Mary Cole Roberts

Comforting words for me, I cannot find.
I know I wrote words for others left behind.
Who's going to write mine?

It's all so new to me. How did I let it get this way?
Why aren't you here to guide me and tell me it's
going to be okay?

I know you trusted me to figure this out.
Without your help, I just feel lost.

Why?

Why are you gone …
and why am I still here?

The Miracle Didn't Come Through

*T*he miracle I was hoping for didn't really come through.
Because as you know, it was that God wouldn't take you.

I didn't pray for it. I felt that was up to him.
And I know why he took you.
You were too tired of fighting…
for every movement and every breath to stay.

I know your final hours were fogged agony.
I know you knew I was with you even then.

I stayed. Helpless to aid. I prayed
and prayed.
Words just flew out.

It didn't change anything.
Peace is now slow to come.

I know you are gone and why.
It still doesn't make it any easier for me now.

And yes, I have discovered how to do many things
you used to do.
I took them for granted … you as well.

Mary Cole Roberts

So much to learn ... don't know if the hours are few or long.

Do know I have to go it alone ... without you.

Oh, God, please guide my steps and tell me what you want me to do.

Oh, Dale, I still miss you.

One Step at a Time

Step One.
Answer. Okay.

Step Two.
Answer. Okay.

Step Three.
Answer. *Okay!*

I am *not* okay. I will *never* be okay again.

But how else do you respond to "How are you?"

Well, I could say …
My heart aches.
My eyes cry.
My life will never be the same again.

It does.
They do.
It won't.

So how do I get past this?

One step at a time … one day at a time … one week
at a time … one step at a time.

Mary Cole Roberts

I Do Not Want
a Testimony

$\mathcal{I}$ do not want a testimony.
I'm giving you one anyway.

I do not want to do this.
Do it anyway.

Don't I have anything to say?
You did. You prayed.

But I prayed for healing.
And what did your husband say?

He said to be careful what I prayed for.
I might not like the answer I get.
And I don't.
Okay.

What do I say? What do I do?
Tell the story of him ... and you.

Okay.

We met. We fell in love.
He got prostate cancer and died ... the end.
It's only the end if I say so.

I still don't know what to do.

Tell the story of him ... and you.

Okay.

You know the saying: when one of you cries, may the other taste the salt?
Yes.
That describes us.

Were you with him when he died?
(Indignantly) Lord, you know the answer to that! (Remorsefully) Standing ... holding his hand as he took his last breath.

What did it feel like?
Like part of me was gone. It still does.

What are you going to do about it?
I don't know.

Have you tried writing?
What do you think I am doing now?

Sigh. Be patient my child. You will find your way.
How do I know I have found my way?

You will know.

It's Hard

I lived more years with you
than I ever did anyone else.
I loved you more than I ever did anyone else.

So what do I do now that I must go on without
you?
How do I face each and every day without you?

I don't know. I am working on it.
And Janie is helping. Is she ever helping.

I try to go to sleep each night as usual after I turn
out the light.

As before, I say my prayers.
I often fall asleep during them.
I hope you are listening.

Sometimes I hear noises the whole night through,
and though I've heard them before,
they are so much louder without you.

I am trying to get the weeds out of the yard.
The heat makes that hard,
coupled with the fact I can still see you ...
sitting on the back porch watching.

Watching just like you did this year when you were too sick to help.

Normal is a state of mind I am not currently in. Yes, I know you want me to continue without you.

It's hard. It's so hard.

There Is a Place

$\mathcal{I}$'m trying to write here. Words won't come.
My mind is a jumble ... words on the run.

As if by appearing, they won't ring true,
won't adequately tell others how I felt about you.

There is a place in the deepest part of my soul
that whispers to me, "You will never again be
whole."

The touch of your hand ... the feel of your face ...
the complete absence of your embrace ...
No one will ever take your place.

I can stare at your picture ... I still don't see you.

I take pride in small accomplishments ...
To Wal-Mart in the truck I went.

I opened Quicken.
At least that's a start,
although I didn't get very far.

I know you laughed out loud at the mess I made ...
when I changed the water in the fish tank.

I re-read the instructions I got off the internet.

Maybe next time, that too, will be an accomplishment.

The flower beds are returning to their normal state.
I still have a bit to go before they once again are their
usual first rate.

I guess I know now why you didn't want to wait ...
until June ...
for them to bloom.

What Next?

Someone should make a checklist of all the things
you need to do ...
when someone else's life is over and the rest is up to
you.

There needs to be some document
to serve as a guide ...
for those of us left behind ...
because we mostly just want to run and hide.

I've been to handling school ... and graduated, too,
but it still didn't prepare me all this to do.

First they put a hold on our financial account.
Now every transaction takes the same circuitous route.
The nervous excuse me ... those waiting, clearing
their throat.
Do they wonder if it's a bad check I wrote?
(as if it's any of their business anyway)

Then to change your social security check, they want
to talk to you.
How they're going to accomplish that, I haven't
got
a clue.

Changing other accounts is about as much fun.
Some want a death certificate (as if I'd lie about it).
Others, *that's okay hon, we'll take your word for it.*

Do they think I made this up as some kind of cruel joke?
Sometimes I think I am going to choke
on all this *fun.*

Being on hold takes hours of my time.

No, you can't do it online.
Come into the office and fill the paperwork out.
I've done that several times now and just want to shout
out loud!

Also, I have filled the paperwork out, only to find
next time that the account is still in your name,
not mine.

Another visit to the office finally got that changed, …
with several clicks on the computer, into my name,
simply because someone I knew
was working the desk that day!

We've had the same credit card account for years.

When I notified them you were deceased, they left me in tears
over what they did next.

Said "I did not have enough experience" with them to merit
the same amount of credit,
so they decreased it by a significant amount.

Some people are helpful; others are solicitous.
None of them know how much I miss ...
you.

This isn't my idea you know.
No one really consulted me.
I guarantee you this is not the way I wanted it to be!

Okay. Here I go.

Breathe.
Breathe again deep.
Rest.
Get some sleep.

Worry about it tomorrow.
What if ...
tomorrow ...
doesn't ...
come?

Missing You

*D*ear Dale,

It's almost the end of the month of July.
My heart still aches. I keep asking myself why?

Why ...
did ...
you ...
die?

I know all the reasons. I truly do.
but that doesn't make me quit missing you.

It's late in the evening and ...
all I have accomplished today ...
is work on the Sands ...
and chart our expenses to date.

Do you remember the gas leak no one else could smell?
It's shut off now ...
Oklahoma Natural Gas obviously could tell.

Thursday the young man was nice as he could be ...
hopefully by Tuesday ... I guess I will see.

Mary Cole Roberts

You know, not having a stove hasn't really bothered me that much ...
don't have any kind of an appetite as such.

No dryer is an inconvenience. No hot water is a different thing.
Cold showers are not as fun as they seemed at Girl Scout camp.

The house is quiet and still ... the neighborhood too.

Dale, my sweetheart, I just wanted you to know I still miss you.

XXOO Mary

Hello. It's me.

Hello. It's me. Your friend Dale E.
I can walk now as far as the eye can see.
Aren't you proud of me?

Yes.

I'm sorry we didn't get to talk the last few days of my life.
Everything was in such a haze to me.
and it was very difficult to breathe.

Okay.

Thank you for letting me go the way I wanted to go.
I know it wasn't easy for you to do that.

No. It wasn't. I have questioned myself every day since.

Well, stop it! I was so tired, …
worn out from what the cancer was
putting my body through.
… but you know I love you.

You told me that.

But do you know that? Really know that?

I think so.

Oh, Mary. You can do so much better than that.

I'll try.

Remember when you told me you loved me the most, the best of all the rest.

Yes.

And I said, "We'll see."

Oh, yes.

Do you see now?

No.

You will.

Always In Your Heart

I don't know what to say to you, my precious pretty wife.
I don't know what you want to hear
now I'm no longer alive.

Yes, you do. Just tell me you love me
and everything is going to be just fine.

Okay.
I love you. Everything's going to be just fine.
Just listen to me.

You will handle this
just like you have handled everything else,
with laughter and a smile.

You'll seek the good among the bad and know you will
be with me in a while.

I see you sitting there, choking back a sob. I know you
are happy I am here
with ...
our ...
God.

And I know how much you miss me. I honestly do.

Mary Cole Roberts

*I know you have many tears, but have cried only a
few.*
I know you can't let them go.

Oh God! I miss you.

*You are figuring it all out just like I knew you could
do,*
*even though part of it, I know you don't really want
to.*

*I see those shoulders shake when you think no one else
sees;*
I know how hard this is to do, alone, without me.

*I hear those keening sounds coming
from your throat,
and recognize the other sounds on which you almost
choke.*

*We've known each other 28 years plus and there were
more than a few
who said it would never last.
Looks like to me, we got the last laugh there, too!*

*That just shows how well they really knew
me
and
you.*

Together we did it always ... never apart.
Friends from the beginning,
then forever in each other's heart.

So let those tears go, privately, if you must.

And let others help you, and in our God, you trust.

It wasn't any easier for me, than it is for you,
except now my pain is gone; my "body" healed;
with freedom I gladly breathe.
And I know I am exactly where he wants me to be.

I know why I am here and someday you will know,
too.

I love you, Mary, and deeply miss you.

I know we are apart now, but I'm never far away.
You must know where I remain.

Always
in your heart.

Mary Cole Roberts

Only You

*G*rief is not a word. It's a process you go through …
when someone you love is "taken" from you.

Some days it is bearable; most days it is not.
You've got to learn to deal with it …
with your head as well as with your heart.

Everything will remind you …
of things you used to do.

Places you used to go …
and go no more.
The Bridge Assembly of God, Primo's, Harry's …
What you used to see …
exploding fireworks, nephews laughing in the
swimming pool, stormy weather …
together.

We cannot go shopping at the mall.
Do you miss that at all?
… visit Durango in the early fall,
go to Cancun *together.*

Together!

There is no more together!
There is no more me and you!
only you.

Mary Cole Roberts

Missing You...
Missing You

Lord are you going to give me the words today?
I still don't know exactly what to say.

The man I lived my life for is now with you ...
and it still affects everything I do.

I can't heal this hurt in my heart.
Where do I begin?
How do I start?

I do not want to waste time shedding these tears
of mine.
So I put on a happy face and hide my tears inside.
Few know; fewer see.

Missing you ...
Dale, missing you.

I make my lists like I always have, mixing the good
in with the bad ...
and doggedly try to resolve the various challenges
I've had.

Getting the car fixed just took time and money.
Good records got a free battery and the truck
running.

The gas line is fixed and the landscaping repairable.
The location of the new meter is bearable.

A lot of the junk we planned to remove
is now hauled off and I know you approve
of all Kevin and I did.

Missing you …
Dale, missing you.

The home repairs will come later,
when it's cooler and others' spare time is greater
than it is now.

Weeding is almost caught up. The rain came.
That's a definite plus.
Quilting looms closer on the horizon.

I can't do this. My heart aches too much.

I Will Always
Love You

I will always love you until the end of time.
You should always know you will forever be mine.

Yes, there may come another. I do not question that.
But he will never take your place.
And you know that for a fact.

God put you and me together for a reason.
Now he has torn us apart.
You will be forever ...
and always ...
in my heart.

I miss you terribly. And I always will.
And I hope you help me as I climb this hill.

I do not know what awaits for me on the other side.
I just trust you ...
and he will function as my guide.

This is most difficult ... an understatement at best.
I do not know exactly how ...
to tackle and master this latest quest.

But he promised to never leave me and be always at my side.
just like he was on the very day that you took your last breath and died.

So now I try to do this without the best part of my life;
but even through all this, I do not question becoming your wife.

Your life on earth is over.
Now you live with the Father and the Son.
And the next part of my life is living, until my life is also done.

I cannot find the words to tell you how much you mean to me,
so may all the poetry I write ...
attempt to convey it so you can still see ...

My heart is aching, completely torn in half.
I truly cannot express ...
just how much ...
I miss your laugh ...
and each and every part of you.

Your wink ...
your mischievous smile ...
your touch too ...

Mary Cole Roberts

your reverence for God ...
your timeliness ...
your gentle clasp ...

But most of all, I miss hearing just from you,
"Hey, Mary, I love you."

Godspeed Dale. I love you, too.

See You Some Day

Hey Sweet Cheeks, it's me. I'm ready! What will it be?

A drive through the countryside or designing a new quilt theme?

I've explored all round heaven; I've seen mom and dad too.
You knew I missed them terribly, didn't you?

We've visited many hours now and I can truly say ...
I never tire of telling them how I love you.

You know you'll see me some day soon.
when it's your turn to be heaven bound.

I know life on earth is difficult for you ...
right now.

I wish there was something I could do to ease your pain.

I'm here for you whenever you want to talk to me.
Just let me know and I'll be right there.

Yes, I miss your touch as much as you miss mine ...

Mary Cole Roberts

and I know that won't change with the passage of time.

Uncle Doug says hello; Aunt Gwen and Willis too.
They all gave me a big "howdy do" when I got here.

I saw your mother's parents; met the other ones too.
They're all proud of you and all you have accomplished.
They said to tell you.

No more struggling for breath; no more pain.

I'm hungry now. I'm ready to eat ...
spaghetti and meat balls, my mother's chocolate cake that she baked.
It tastes just like I remember it did.
I guess the chocolate rum cake will have to wait until you get here.

Mary, I sure miss you.

I know your poetry is your release ...
for all those tears you keep stored inside;
and honey, though you believe the tears are a private thing,
don't keep them choked off or they won't cease.

Someday, they will flood when you least expect it ...
and I don't want you to be that upset.

You tell Taylor, Tanner too,

I miss them almost as much as I miss you.

From here I can still watch them growing up.

By the way, I'm proud you sold the truck to Tay.
I can't think of anyone I'd rather have it.

You really need to set this aside and get some rest.
Yes, I know you've tried. Just do your best.

That's all anyone can ask of you.

Our yard looks pretty good.
Yes, I see the mess.
It will grow back …
almost before you know it.

I know you struggled when you had to remove the pentagon bed.
Honey, it's been dead a long time.
It will be okay to replace it.

I love this place.
You will find it worth the wait.

There's no limit to what I can do.
Sugar, I miss you. See you someday.

It won't be anytime soon.

Mary Cole Roberts

What Do I Do With My Wedding Ring?

*W*hat do I do with my wedding ring?
I've worn it forever and always, it seems.

Now that my husband is no longer around.
Tho' it's true—in heaven he can be found.

What do I do with it?
I feel undressed without it.
Totally naked without it.

So I am actually living a lie ...
wearing it on the third finger of my left hand as always.

Yes, I know ... he ... died.
So what?

Thanks, but you don't need to remind me of the cold hard truth.

I've worn my ring daily for almost twenty-eight years.
Years of joyful, blissful happiness. Few tears.

My left hand looks weird without that mixed band of diamonds, silver, and gold.

Actually it grabs at my heart, my very soul ...
not to see it circled there.
My heart cries out, "Does anyone else care?"

When is it time to remove it ... forever?
"Better or worse ... richer or poorer ... "
This certainly isn't better!

What do I do with my wedding ring ...
now that he's gone.

Make it gone too?

Mary Cole Roberts

What I Wanted It For

$\mathcal{J}$ thought my own words were different ...
but they're a lot the same.

The only thing that's different
is the pain from which they came.

Or is the pain the same?
I haven't finished the little book yet.
It's still too soon, too painful for me to read.
I didn't really think I was all alone ...
just that no one else could see.

Losing you has not really
settled down to acceptance yet ...
although I do know you are gone.
It's just like something's missing,
and my mind's a bit fogged.

Others' words affect me still.
Of course, that's no different than before.

I wanted this dance for the rest of my life.
I got it for the rest of yours.

What I wanted it for was the rest of mine.

The Caregiver

$\mathcal{I}$ am a caregiver. It's just something I naturally do.
But when a caregiver needs a caregiver, how do you find one for you?

The trust is done; the papers will soon be filed.
So how many more miles do I walk before I see you?
I have no earthly idea.

How do you find a caregiver for you?

Do you search the yellow pages?
Read a book?
Search out the route others took?
Withdraw. Run away.

Mary, my dear wife, you can't withdraw—that's not your way.
Otherwise you wouldn't have made it to get here today.

You listen to your heart and others' thoughts as well…
and stumble along…
until you find the right path…
and take it.

Mary Cole Roberts

The Truck

*H*ey honey! It's me, your Mary!

The driveway looks empty, oh so empty today
with only one vehicle occupying space.

Your F150 pickup you loved so much now belongs
to Tay,
and will receive his special touch,
instead of yours.

He seemed very pleased,
but didn't get to enjoy it much initially ...
as we had to load the trailer so Kevin could leave
right after his meeting the next day.

I know you could see, probably lots better than
me ...
how we decorated it for Tay to see.

He didn't even know it was for sale ...
or would have suspected, I know.
It was so hard for me ... and Kevin ... and April ...
not to tell.

It will make him a good truck ... not one he has to
fix up.

That will allow him to concentrate on other things...
such as filling it up with gasoline.

I left the small bag of tools, the bungee cords, the rope too;
told him I would make new towels if he so chooses.

He needs time to think on things like that and decide...
at some point in the future.

He has other traits like me (well, actually his dad)...
no tolerance for incompetence...
wants to be way early, never late.

I told him everyone couldn't be perfect like him and me.
He said he wasn't...
I told him that's the point...
He said, "Oh, I see."

This time, he, not his mom,
did ask me if I would come
to watch and listen to him drum.

To say I was surprised...
at the request...
is an understatement at best.

This teenage nephew,
with whom we have been blessed,
made me feel special, so yes ...

I went.

All the instruments in the "drumline," he explained.
No, I don't remember, but, yes, he gave me each of
their names,
and exactly how they fit into the overall scheme.
The finished sound of That Altus Band, I mean.
Yes, I went.

I will go back.

I Found Your Lucky Parking Spot

I found your lucky parking spot across from the cart drop at Sam's ...
then again at Penney's when I went to find out what size I am.
(I still don't know—I didn't find anything today.)

Your computer misses you. I do too.
It's trying to like me. I'm trying to like it too.

I am facing a lot of firsts in life. (Cheryl is as well.)
Somehow those firsts are different now ... more poignant than before.

I know how she is doing. Okay. Just like you.

The Caddo men came out today. They marked their line.
When will the others be here, theirs to find?

Sometime.

I am working on Daddy's quilt ... have all but the last border done.
That makes one more ready to quilt.

How many do you have now?

Mary Cole Roberts

I don't really know, but I promise I will get to it.

I know you will, soon.

Those pills I had trouble with most of the year worked.

No problems showed.

Good.

What's it like?
What do you mean?
You know what I mean!
(chuckle) Yes I do.

It's more beautiful than I ever imagined.

I know you read about heaven's size in some of the literature everyone has been giving you.
Yes.

By the way, Mom and Dad say hi.
Hi back ... but you still haven't answered me.

Honey, the beauty of heaven is indescribable.
The flowers are more vivid hues than you have ever seen.
We all have our assignments to do. (I chose you.)

I guess no more pain and no more need for drugs is the most important part.

We are all happy here, but I still miss you. You need to remember that.

I do. I miss you too.

The CD in the Truck

I see you found the cd in my pickup truck ...
and remembered I like to listen to my music loud.

I know you know I picked the music for the beat, not
the words they speak.

Yes, I even heard the bass notes hit their peak.
And, yes, I enjoyed it ... and you know why.
It's the very last one you made
before you died.

I saw you tear up. I saw you cry.
I know you don't do it much ...
and I know you are very sad I died.

So here's a wink from me to you ...
one just like I used to do.

A hug and a kiss too ...

I'm thinking about you.

You Knew

Your side of the bed is smooth and unrumpled …
just waiting for you to come a bit later …
like you used to do.

Except it still looks the same the next morning.
Lord, how I miss you! I miss you!

In the hospital, you told me where to find
the combination to the safe … the numbers
written down, but not the turns.

You knew! You knew! I didn't know, but you knew!

You pulled out the feeding tube. The doctor didn't
replace it.

He knew! You knew!

The choice we didn't have to make of where to
go …

He knew! You knew! I was in denial.

It was still another week.

I miss you! God, how I miss you!

Mary Cole Roberts

Would You?

$\mathcal{J}$f I stayed in the house
and never came out,
would losing you be easier to do?

If I never darkened the doors of the church;
just watched the daylight hours merge
into night, would losing you be easier to do?

If I stayed in bed,
pulled the covers up over my head,
would losing you be easier to do?
I see you are justifiably horrified
to my reaction to the fact you died.

Actually, this has not been my reaction at all.
I know in my heart it's not
what you would have wanted me to do.
You would have wanted me to stand tall
and face it all, ... head on.

I write ... I plan ... I visit ... I shop ... I read ... I
pine.
You see, the memory of you is never quite out of
my mind.

I handle our problems, and many they have been.
I always try solving them alone.
Every now and then, someone else has to lend
a helping hand.

The list is getting longer of the things
I have to do.
… the things I have to do without you.

I know this is the way it's supposed to be.
Oh, why didn't God take me …
instead of you?

Would you have been able to do this alone
without me?
I would have expected you to.

Just like you expect me to do.

Mary Cole Roberts

I Miss

$\mathcal{J}$ miss the warmth of being cuddled up next to you at night ...

the feeling of your touch ever so light ...

the sound of your voice that made everything right ...

the smile you brought to everyone in sight.

I miss the fact that you fought with all your might ...

until it was time to give up the fight ...

so God could heal your body on new heights ...

when he called you home forever more.

I Planned Ahead

I planned ahead. I brought a dress.
Actually, I planned to wear it to church Sunday.
I don't want to wear it to the funeral.

I brought my poetry to double check.
I only opened it to share the first one ...
for my momma.

Everyone is here or will be here except you.
All those in my life who count are here except you.

I could list them all, but I know you and Momma
see.
I miss both of you terribly.
My emotions are raw, on edge, uncontrolled.
This was so soon after yours.
How do I do this one too?

Tears flow ...
freely ...
freely flow.

Everyone's crying buckets of tears.

Mary Cole Roberts

Tomorrow will be hard ... Monday worse.
There is something called a viewing.
(I think Catholics call it a wake.)

I don't want to stand there in that tiny room ...
with her and everyone and all the flowers.

I can't do this.
I can't take this.
This is too soon.

To Dale:
Valentine's Day, 2004

*M*y husband, you're a good man and I just want
you to know
I'm here with you, beside you wherever you go.

Our years are multiplying, our idiosyncrasies too;
other things may change, but never my love for
you.

To say that I cherish my moments with you,
and that I'm looking forward to more of them, too,
is an understatement at best;
but you do know what I mean when I say ...
all the rest don't hold a candle to you.
Our lifestyle may change, our friends too, but
never, ever, my love for you.

I am proud to call you my husband.
You must be a part of God's plan for me.
I know he couldn't have chosen a finer man than
you.

If there are days when the weight of the world is
getting you down,

Mary Cole Roberts

may the thought of my love make a smile of that
inward frown.

May you never doubt the depths of my feelings for
you.
You should truly know I will always love you.
From this day forward "til death
do us part" is written
forever deep in my heart

So on this Valentine's Day, 2004, know that I love
you this much and more
and I'm ready for whatever our life has in store.

We'll face it together, two as one ...
living ... loving ... laughing ...
always with fun,
until God says we're done.

I love you Dale! Happy Valentine's Day 2004!

How Do I Love You?

How do I love you—let me count the ways.

Those are someone else's words ...
and I want my own to say ...
that I love you more than this much,
more than you breathe or eat,
even when you're angry or only fast asleep.

I love you higher than birds can soar ...
and more than any words can say.

That's what I'm trying to tell you ...
on this Valentine's Day.

I love you taller than my garden weeds can grow ...
and deeper than the deepest snow;
better than the best chocolate ...
you ever ate;
more than the widest chasm ...
better than the fastest heart rate.

I love you more than yesterday,
less than tomorrow,
more than I can really say.

Mary Cole Roberts

And that's what I'm trying to tell you ...
on this Valentine's Day.

I love you the mostest ...
the best ...
of all the rest.

More than mere words can say.

That's what I *am* telling you
on this Valentine's Day.

You Are My Husband

You are my husband, the light of my life.
I thank God for the day you made me your wife.

For richer, for poorer, where else do we stand?
Walking together, hand in hand.

Though the years may bring changes all around
us ...
the two of us remain true to each other, a definite
plus.

How many years have gone by?
Seems like only a blink of an eye.

But I have known you forever and ever!
Amen.
Don't even remember a time before then.

May you know I am very proud of you ...
all you accomplish, all you do.

And I will always be here waiting for you ...
ready to do whatever you want to do.

Mary Cole Roberts

And yes, every now and then I will sneak in some
of my own stuff
listening for your laughter, reaching for your touch.

At night when we sleep, all cuddled up tight ...
I thank the Lord above for you with all my might.

Sometimes you lying there, I see ...
sleeping peacefully, as quiet as can be.
And once again, I thank God, you *chose* me.

And I know you have dreams, and cares too,
and I hope I fit into all that you do.

May you know I love you; I try to always make
you first.
Our love is forever a blessing, never a curse.

My life is complete as never before ...
and I will love you forever and ever more.

I wish you a Happy Anniversary, dear husband.
I love you more than the all the rest of them.

I will love you always until the end!

Addendum

In February, I knew in my heart we would not beat the prostate cancer this time.

I knew, but I ignored all the warning signs. As if I would have recognized them anyway; what exactly were they?

Praying for healing must not have been the right prayer to pray. I prayed it anyway. Even after a friend told me I needed to pray for a miracle.

If God wanted us to have a miracle, he would have given us one. He gave us healing—not the healing I wanted, but the healing Dale needed.

My body cringes every time I remember the doctor's description of the catheter banging to and fro in his body. Every time his body was moved it banged. It had to be an absolute agony.

Dale wanted me to stay at the hotel so I would be closer. It was a nice, quiet hotel room; he knew the phone number. He had no grasp of night or day, only that I was gone and he wanted to see me.

I would get dressed and go see him—lying there in that hospital bed, the room lights still on even in the middle of the night.

He didn't notice I had on no makeup or that my hair was pulled back tightly. He saw me and was happy and began to rest again.

One time he apologized for calling me "at a God awful hour of the morning." I told him it didn't matter. It didn't. I kissed him and told him I loved him.

If he wanted to talk to me or see me several times at night when I was trying to sleep, it wouldn't have mattered. It wouldn't have mattered.

Often, I had great difficulty sleeping. I still do. I developed a habit of calling the nurses station to check on him if I woke up.

June tenth, I awoke at 1:30 a.m. and called. He was awake; the call was transferred to his room. His sister Anita was still there with him. Her plane to return home was around six a.m.

"Are you ready for me to come up?"

"*Yes. How soon will you be here?*"

"About three."

"*Okay. I love you. See you then.* "

I got there shortly after 2:30 am. Anita asked if I wanted her to stay. I said no. In my mind, Dale and I needed time alone—just each other. I kissed Dale hello.

"I love you."

"*I love you, too. Don't put me back on that machine.*"

"But it helps you breathe better."

"*I don't want back on it.*"

"Okay. I won't. Nita said you were in pain."

"*Yes.*"

"Let's get you some pain medication."

"*Okay.*"

As the nurse administered the shot, Nita and I both heard him say, "*Nooooo.*"

She left for the hotel to pack.

I pulled the chair over to the bed and took his hand. He went to sleep. I went to sleep.

The doctor arrived. "*Why isn't he on the BiPap?*"

"He said he didn't want back on it."

"*He won't make it through the day without it.*"

With an ominous lump in my throat, I said, "I can't. I told him I wouldn't."

While holding my husband's hand, I sat and wrote. Through my tears and a choking voice, I read him the Twenty-third Psalm. I wrote. I wrote some more. My friend Cheryl brought Panera Bread for lunch. We stayed right there, ate, and visited a short while. Dale slept.

All this time, he was on an oxygen cannula.

His heart rate was slowing. I could see it. I knew. I still didn't believe he was dying.

When everyone else came by, I can't exactly tell you. But there was Connie and Janie and Brother Ken.

His blood pressure began to drop. I saw it. I knew. I was beginning to believe. David, the respiration therapist who had been so good and patient with Dale, came into the room.

Almost panicky, David said, "*I need to put him back on the BiPap.*"

"You can't. I told him I wouldn't," I said.

"*I've got to get him more oxygen.*"

"Do what you have to do—no BiPap."

All of Dale's vitals were dropping. The room began filling with nurses; I couldn't look at their faces. Their movements give them away; more machines come in. My husband was leaving this world.

Brother Ken had just been at Baptist Hospital for the birth of his granddaughter and was headed home. Something made him turn around and come to see Dale, although he had just been there on Monday. I know who made him turn around. God did.

Janie, Brother Ken, and I were back away from

the foot of the bed—truly trying to stay out of everyone's way; standing and talking. I couldn't even tell you what anyone was saying.

In an urgent voice, David said, "*Pastor! Pastor, it's time.*"

Brother Ken took Dale's and Janie's hands. I had Janie's and Dale's. Everyone else disappeared. At the time, I felt peace and relief for my precious husband. I can't tell you any of the prayer. I know Dale heard it. I don't doubt that. He took his last jagged breath and died. I hugged and kissed my baby goodbye. "I will love you forever," I said.

CC, our next door neighbor came in. She was very upset. I talked to her.

I heard the doctor's footsteps coming down the hallway. He gently spoke directly to me and told me Dale was with Jesus now. I stepped back away from the bed so the doctor could do his job.

I couldn't believe Dale was gone. I knew he was gone. I just couldn't believe it. I asked for his hospital identification bracelets. I still carry them in my purse. I wear a gold heart on a gold chain around my neck. It is the first present he ever gave me. Whenever either of us traveled and we had to sleep apart, I never took it off until we slept together again. It's there today.

I work in the yard. I eat sometimes. I see some close friends. I take care of business—the business Dale took care of all our married life. I handle crisis—the crisis Dale handled all our married life. I cry alone. Tears are private. They do fall sometimes in the presence of others, but not often. I write. I read. I quilt. Most of all, I miss my precious husband. Goodbye, Dale. Godspeed.

Endnotes

1   1 Peter 5:7; Philippians 4:6–7; II Chronicles 20:15, Proverbs 3:5

listen|imagine|view|experience

AUDIO BOOK DOWNLOAD INCLUDED WITH THIS BOOK!

In your hands you hold a complete digital entertainment package. Besides purchasing the paper version of this book, this book includes a free download of the audio version of this book. Simply use the code listed below when visiting our website. Once downloaded to your computer, you can listen to the book through your computer's speakers, burn it to an audio CD or save the file to your portable music device (such as Apple's popular iPod) and listen on the go!

How to get your free audio book digital download:

1. Visit www.tatepublishing.com and click on the e|LIVE logo on the home page.
2. Enter the following coupon code:
   7243-ea83-502a-d467-2141-7604-efcd-3480
3. Download the audio book from your e|LIVE digital locker and begin enjoying your new digital entertainment package today!

ROUGH
PATCHES

Navigating Marital Hard Spots

Francie Taylor

Copyright © 2017 by Francie Taylor
Published by Keep the Heart
Apple Valley, Minnesota 55124
www.keeptheart.com

978-0-9989009-0-2

Cover design by Keep the Heart, LLC

Scripture quotations are taken from the King James Version of the Bible.

CONTENTS

ACKNOWLEDGMENTS

To my Lord and Saviour, Jesus Christ: Thank You for the life-altering gift provided by salvation. Without the Word of God, all my relationships would be in total disarray.

To my Norman H. Taylor: Thank you for loving me as "Christ loved the church." And thank you for eating so much chicken…again.

To our adult children, Austen and Jessica (the "other" Mr. and Mrs. Taylor), Hillary, and Collin: Thank you for the joy that you all bring to our lives.

To my dear sister friend, Vikki Pierson: Thank you for your encouragement, valuable input and proofreading services. You made significant contributions to this manuscript.

To our Team of Proofreaders, Heather Bomstad, Jessica Taylor, and Angie Zachary: Thank you for providing "extra eyeballs" and immensely relevant feedback.

To my Team of Reviewers: To those who took the time

during a very busy season to read the preview copy, thank you for your reviews.

To my "Almost Twin" Sis, Janelle Danforth: Thank you for always reading my "idea emails." I owe you some Key Lime pie on our next trip to the seashore.

To our webmaster, John Hooper, at www.gohooper.com: Hoop, thanks so much for helping us get this project onto the website at Keep the Heart.

To Linda Stubblefield: Thank you for your gifted and professional assistance with this booklet. You took what seemed like an overwhelming task and brought it to completion. You are gifted and your work is beautiful.

The Lord has filled my life with some very precious people. Thank you all.

REVIEWS

Mrs. Tonia Tewell—Theodore, Alabama

One of my first thoughts was this: "Francie Taylor got so mad she threw a box of tissues?! She's human!" Why are we so stubborn and prideful that we can't allow God's word to penetrate our hearts and fix what needs to be fixed? It starts with ME! I cried...so much wisdom shared with God's Word as the guide for all this instruction. It all starts with MY choices in obeying God's instructions. This amazing booklet is packed with so much wisdom, but short enough for a quick read. It's like we're having a "Sister, I love you" talk.

Mrs. Pam Brown—Livonia, Michigan

Years ago I heard a preacher say, "Life is 10% of what happens to you, and 90% of how you respond to it." The same could be said about our marriages. Francie's booklet, Rough Patches, offers some helpful, practical and Scriptural answers. Our sister friend reminds us that our right responses to the "rough patches" that inevitably will invade our lives and marriages, can make the difference between a thriving relationship rather than one that is simply surviving.

Mrs. Angie Zachary—San Diego, California

With her usual no-nonsense approach, Francie Taylor has packed this little booklet full of Bible-based truths that will help any married couple navigate troubled waters… and also avoid some of the storms that cause them!

Mrs. Renee Cox, Durham, North Carolina

This excellent, brief booklet addresses problems most of us deal with from a very practical and biblical stand-point. It feels like the author is spending time with me as I read this booklet, and I am helped by that. Thank you, Francie Taylor, for your words of wisdom and straightfor-ward approach to these sensitive subjects.

Mrs. Patty Boyle—Spokane, Washington

As I was reading Francie Taylor's new booklet, *Rough Patches*, I was thinking, "Where was this booklet 42 years ago when I was saying 'I Do'"? *Rough Patches* is a very prac-tical help with answers from God's Word. Francie's humor and transparency makes you feel comfortable as you read real answers to real problems. I highly recommend this booklet as a resource for marriages in any stage of love.

Mrs. Becky Earnhart—Grand Blanc, Michigan

Rough Patches simply yet directly addresses real-life challenges in every marriage. Even couples that have waited for God to send the right mate into their life, maintained their purity throughout dating, and dedicated themselves to live for God have seasons of struggles. There are days when that "amazing mate" doesn't look so amazing. You know that you love them; you're just not so sure if you like them anymore! There are universal struggles in any marriage relationship. There is hope…there can be healing and restoration.

Grab a cup of coffee (or sweet tea!) and enjoy a conversation with Francie as she shares from a heart of wisdom and experience. She will answer some of the questions you're afraid to ask!

Sonya Williams—Long Island, New York

I couldn't put the booklet down. I read this booklet in two sittings with a cup of coffee, nodding in agreement the whole time. *Rough Patches* is simple to read and easy to understand, just like God's Word. I felt this booklet was written to ME, a wife in this generation, who faces real marital issues every single day. I found answers to those issues with three simple words: *shift, edit,* and *handle.* I felt like my heart did a swan-dive into a pool of peace. One quote from the booklet that stuck with me is this: "…a storm-free life is merely an optical illusion." I was reminded throughout this booklet that marital peace, hope, and long-suffering patience is possible when handle our marriages through prayer and submission to God's awesome plan. My heart was lifted.

Shelly Hamilton—Greenville, South Carolina

We know there are rough patches in every marriage, but there are ways to work through these times. I agree with her assessment of staying out of the "negative loop" in how we think about our husbands. We all need to focus on the wonderful reasons why we married our men in the first place. May your treatment of your husband be a shining light to a lost world.

Janice Wolfe—Evansville, Indiana

Nearly 20 years ago Dan and I blended our two families. Seven children in all!! You might say there have been a few "rough patches" along the way. It has been godly advice like you'll find in this booklet that has helped us through our journey of love and oneness. Francie inspires us as she instructs us. Great read!

Cindie Trieber—Santa Clara, California

My husband and I have been in the ministry for over four decades, and we have counseled hundreds of couples before marriage, and during every stage of marriage. Marriage is a journey, and every journey has *Rough Patches*. One definition Webster gives for the word *patch* is "a period of time." Christ does not expect us to *endure* our marriage, but rather to *enjoy* our marriage. The wisdom and advice written in the pages of this booklet should be mandatory reading for all couples. You will be greatly helped not only by reading it, but also by applying it to your marriage.

Mrs. Loretta Walker, Roundup Ministries

As I reviewed Francie's new booklet, *Rough Patches*, I was busily preparing for my daughter to be married. While reading, I kept thinking, "I can't wait to buy this for Jeannie." Francie captured my attention by intertwining real-life illustrations with lots of Scripture. The pointed statements and questions forced me to evaluate my own marriage. One of them was this: "Are we making our husbands' lives more favorable with our presence?" *That* hit me right between the running lights! This very convicting booklet is sure to make your marriage better, but what I loved the most is she gives us practical ways to fix the problems. I ended the booklet encouraged.

Mrs. Linda Wilkerson, Hammond, Indiana

In five well-written, well-versed chapters, Francie Taylor addresses conflict head on and shows how to navigate marital challenges. Have you ever heard the words, "The honeymoon's over"? Those words are not made in reference to newlyweds arriving home from their honeymoon! They are expressed when a conflict has reared its ugly head and reconciliation seems hopeless. Francie teaches how to communicate effectively, how to recognize and meet each other's needs, and that walking with God is vital.

Pastor David Clear—First Baptist Church, Rosemount, Minnesota

Here in Minnesota, our wintry weather often brings challenging road surfaces—namely ice and snow. When the road surface changes, it is easy to get out of control. Almost all marriages encounter "rough patches," and like vehicles in wintry weather; it is always wise to get yourself under control quickly. In this booklet, Francie Taylor has laid out easy-to-follow instructions helping wives to do just that. I loved the simple instructions that help wives (and this would also be good for husbands) to have a Spirit-controlled response to marital "curve balls." The wisdom she shares is invaluable. *(Note: Pastor Clear is Norm and Francie Taylor's Pastor and friend.)*

INTRODUCTION

I HOPE YOU REALIZE that working on a booklet about marriage is enough to cause an argument. Suddenly, instead of just living our marriage, we're putting it under the microscope for closer analysis. Guess what happens next? A moment of tension becomes double-pressure as we remember that we're working on a booklet about marriage! But we are also fully aware that a flawed couple lives in this home, so we know better than to expect marital perfection. If Bibles had pictures next to the verses, ours would be next to this one: *"As it is written, There is none righteous, no, not one..."* (Romans 3:10) We said "I do" over three decades ago, but we are still figuring out what that means. We have learned quite a bit about what works, but we know even more about what *doesn't* work.

I have been married to my Norman H. Taylor since 1982. Does that make me an expert? No, but I do know a bit about rough patches. In fact, while working on this project, I had a flashback to a time when I was so incredibly angry at my Norman H. that I threw a tissue box at the wall (in his direction). It exploded and the tissues flew all over the place. The look in my husband's eyes was not one of amusement.

It was a failed attempt at conflict resolution. Understatement.

I have since learned that calm and timely discussions wrapped in prayer and patience are far more effective. It also helps to listen carefully with a goal of understanding the other person, not merely to formulate the next reply. Too many people talk over each other, rarely even considering what has been said.

What do we want—long and happy marriages or short and turbulent endurance matches? We do want things to work out in our marriages, don't we?

This booklet briefly outlines how a shift in perspective coupled with an appropriate response can help us to handle matters wisely, ultimately leading to a better outcome. And when I say "better outcome," I don't mean free of pain or sorrow; this simply means that we'll be relying on God's wisdom rather than our own methods.

You'll see the following words at the end of each brief chapter: *Shift, Edit,* and *Handle Wisely.* Here's what these terms mean:

Shift the perspective:
Is there another way to view the issue?

Edit the response:

Is there a gentler tone or more effective method that can be employed?

Handle matters wisely:

Are we even pausing long enough to pray, or are we just plowing ahead without consulting the Lord?

Although some couples may get off to a rocky start, many have an enjoyable entry into married life. The rough patches tend to come later, after the gift cards have all been spent and the wedding glow has worn off. In fact, some couples go for decades without any major difficulties, when suddenly, they hit a crisis and things quickly become stressful. Thankfully, our situations are not too rugged for the Lord, even though they may seem desperate to us.

When it comes to enduring rough patches, wisdom is more important than endurance. With God's wisdom, strength is preserved as we avoid expending energy on unnecessary emotions and improperly resolved conflicts.

> *"How much better is it to get wisdom*
> *than gold! and to get understanding*
> *rather to be chosen than silver!"*
> Proverbs 16:16

ONE

TRAPPED IN A NEGATIVE LOOP

"He that is first in his own cause seemeth just; but his neighbour cometh and searcheth him."

(Proverbs 18:17)

M ANY PROBLEMS IN marriage stem from a "me first" perspective. It's common to view things from our side first, but "common" is not the same as "correct."

I asked a young wife this question during a mentoring session: "How long has it been since you've said something pleasant to your husband?"

The young woman looked up, as if trying hard to recall a time. A few seconds passed before she said, "I can't remember. It's been years."

Years?

I asked a follow-up question: "Would you want to live with someone like you?"

"No!" she said emphatically.

All I could do was nod.

When a couple gets trapped in a negative loop, there is a great risk of it becoming the only operating system that they know. One person says something negative, so the other person tries to "one-up" them, saying something equally harsh if not worse.

In other cases, instead of words flying, the silent treatment may be used as a weapon of retaliation.

Either way, it's not long before coldness sets in.

When two married people are getting along worse than two despised roommates in a college dorm room, things have gotten out of hand and need repair. Married people have managed to stay married while mistreating each other for years, but is that your goal?

People tend to slide into negative habits when they've had a string of negative experiences that have piled up as unresolved conflicts.

Ask yourself this question: When did the negative loop start in your marriage? What was the trigger? Was there ever a time when things were pleasant between you, or have you been struggling since day one? While it helps if you can identify the root, sometimes the main thing that is needed is change.

If no one is willing to stop being negative, both sides will remain stuck. Before long, anger turns to bitterness, and the root of bitterness spreads a viral contaminant throughout the entire home. From the outside, we may be able to put a bright face on the marriage; but behind closed doors, it's dark.

When things are in a bad place, we look for someone to blame. It's human nature. And it's never one person's fault alone. Two people said "I do," so when there's a problem, two people have problems together. In fact, if we want to be technical about it, since the husband and wife become "one flesh" on the wedding day, it could be said that one couple has problems.

It's so easy to look at the other person and itemize their faults. The better option is to first take a look at what can be done to improve our side of the situation.

Do we need to improve our tone? *"A soft answer turneth away wrath: but grievous words stir up anger."* (Proverbs 15:1) Sometimes, developing the habit of editing our own words eventually leads to improved communications on both sides.

Are we unpleasant company? *"Let her be as the loving hind and pleasant roe…"* (Proverbs 5:19a) When our husbands are hurting, they need compassion, just like we do. You may wonder, "But what if he's never compassionate towards me?" We will never improve a situation by engaging in unpleasantness. What if Christ had decided that we weren't worth dying for because we lacked the character qualities that He possessed?

Are we making our husbands' lives more favorable with our presence? *"Whoso findeth a wife findeth a good thing, and obtaineth favour of the LORD."* (Proverbs 18:22)

By now, you may even feel like all the blame is being placed at your feet while your husband just gets away with being a big negative crab. Not so.

We're looking at the wife's side of the equation. This is not about who wins the prize for "most faults." We are learning how to take wise Scriptural steps towards conflict resolution. And even if we've done all that we can do, we may still have to patiently wait on the Lord while He does "heart surgery" on our beloved husbands.

Marriage is not a drive-through window; it's slow cooking. If we'll pay attention to the ingredients that we're adding to our married lives, it will take the focus off what we may consider faults. We can't control our husbands. Have you learned that by now? But the good news is this: we can control our responses to them.

SHIFT: Yield.

If you love your beloved, you will yield your desire to have him be someone different. He is who he is, and even though he may need to change, there is always enough of that need to go around. Have you considered yielding your picture of the ideal husband to the Lord and leaving it there?

EDIT: Pray.

Ask the Lord to heal whatever is broken. Something is wrong with a person who is stuck in a negative loop.

"But I HAVE PRAYED," you may be thinking. Never stop praying.

Search your own heart as well, and ask the Lord to reveal areas that need improvement. And remember, the changes you may be praying for are not just for your husband; it's also in how you view your situation. God always sees more clearly than we see. This is not to minimize or downplay the pressure of how hard things are, but if we only focus on the hardness, we may miss the valuable lessons wrapped in the package. Three words make up a pivotal verse:

"Pray without ceasing." (1 Thessalonians 5:17)

HANDLE WISELY: Resolve.

Would you love your husband if he never changes from the stuck spot he is in right now? Prove it. Resolve from this day forward to love him just as he is, the same way Christ loves us.

*"Whoso keepeth his mouth
and his tongue
keepeth his soul from troubles."*
(Proverbs 21:23)

Two

COUNSEL

"He that answereth a matter before he heareth it, it is folly and shame unto him." (Proverbs 18:13)

KEEP THE HEART has a Facebook page, and we often receive requests via private messages for counsel. Unfortunately, we are unable to provide counsel in this way. The problem is this: we would become "counselors to the World Wide Web" without really knowing if we're even close to giving beneficial guidance.

The Bible tells us that it's foolish to attempt to answer something before we've even gathered all the facts. Giving counsel without understanding is silly at best; harmful at worst.

Why are people so reluctant to seek counsel? I've heard a few of the reasons, but certainly there are more than these:

- Not wanting others to know that there are problems
- Not comfortable with the counselors available in the area
- A deep desire to maintain an image that things are fine

I've said it before and will repeat it often: It's not a shame to need counsel; it's a shame to need it and refuse to get it.

Here are some situations that may indicate a need for counseling:

1) **Addictions.** This is such a complicated issue, and trying to navigate an addiction problem without help may result in prolonged pain and deeper problems in the long run. Whether it's addiction to drugs, alcohol, or even food, outside help may provide the accountability that is often missing, among other things.

2) **Infidelity.** Unfortunately, there are many marriages that are destroyed by the tidal waves of pain that often accompany the betrayal of infidelity. If possible and if reasonable, seek godly counsel before seeking a lawyer.

3) **Abuse.** Physical, emotional and verbal abuses are forms of cruelty that are often hidden from view, but existing in homes that give the appearance of being "normal." If you are suffering from abuse, counsel is essential. Waiting could actually be hazardous to you and others. Get help promptly.

4) **Serious neglect.** When a couple stops communicating, the marriage relationship is being neglected. How can two people expect to stay together if they're not even speaking to each other? Something

is broken, and counsel is essential. Do not continue in this condition.

5) **Depression.** Sometimes too many things go wrong all at once, causing a person to slide from discouragement to despair, and ultimately, to depression. Never be ashamed to get help for depression. Whether it's for a short season or a long period of time, counsel provides needed support.

People may wonder where to turn for counsel. Whenever possible, ask your pastor. If your pastor is not available, ask him for a referral. This is a starting point, but you may need more help than your church can provide, or you may need outside help if you are a pastor's wife. If this is the case, you will need to seek help from a qualified Christian counselor in your area. Discreetly ask for a referral from a trusted godly Christian.

Many Christian counseling centers offer their services on a sliding scale, making it affordable. It may help to start from scratch with someone who is listening without the back-story of "knowing your family from church." The main point is this: if you need counsel, please seek it before things get worse.

SHIFT: No more pretending.

If you truly want to work for improvement, the first step is to give up the make-believe marriage and put that effort into building a healthy marriage. It's also vital to remember that people do care about you, and they may even be able to tell that you're struggling as a couple, but they may not help unless you ask. You don't have to pretend to be fine when you're not.

EDIT: Limit words.

When a couple is already hurting, the more they argue and play the "blame game," the worse things may become. Be sure to limit the words that you speak while you're in the process of engaging in counsel. *"In the multitude of words there wanteth not sin: but he that refraineth his lips is wise."* (Proverbs 10:19) There is no sense in talking yourself into more strife.

HANDLE WISELY: Use discretion.

Some women tell way too many people about their marital problems, while others won't tell a soul. Both ways are lacking balance. Just as it is important to seek counsel to handle the more complicated issues, it is just as vital not to tell too many people about your private matters. One day, the two of you could be just fine again. Do you really need to have a dozen people knowing the blow-by-blows of your struggles? Keep this between you and the trusted, small circle of counselors.

THREE

CHALLENGES FROM CHILDREN

"A foolish son is a grief to his father, and bitterness to her that bare him." (Proverbs 17:25)

THIS CHAPTER WAS originally titled, "Children Dropping Bombs," but that sounded too negative. To be fair, we're not on the minds of our children when they're coming up with their surprises. In fact, whenever possible, many children will hide bad news. But it's amazing how "hidden things" behave like bombs on timers with detonators attached.

Children don't intend to drop bombs. They're busy living and trying to figure things out, and sometimes this presents challenges that they process differently than we would. You may also have noticed that young people asking for guidance is uncommon during times like these.

Here's a list of announcements that may hit us hard:

- "I'm pregnant."
- "I'm gay."
- "I'm in jail."
- "I'm marrying this person I just met..."

- "I'm moving out to live with my boyfriend/girl-friend."
- "I'm not going to church anymore."
- "I don't believe in God…"

The stress and grieving that follows unfortunate news has a way of bringing pressure to the marriage. After all, fathers process conflicts differently than mothers do, and our children are well aware of this. If you don't think so, notice who usually gets the phone calls.

Mom. Sometimes Dad, but more often, Mom is the first call. Regardless of who gets the news first, remember that it's more important that we have a proper response.

You are not the first parent to receive disappointing news from a child. You may feel "alone" in your experience, and maybe you don't personally know anyone in a similar strait, but you're still not the first.

This is not the time to write off your child. Love your children always.

This is not the time to start sniping at your husband. Love your husband always.

This is not the time to accuse or blame God or Christianity. Love God always.

If you have other children, remember that they are observing your reactions and responses. Staying unified as a family is pivotal to managing the situation.

Sit down with your husband and pray, then plan. Be

sure that the family hears reassuring words like, "We're going to get through this together with the Lord." Most of all, remind yourself that while your physical world has been shaken, God was not caught by surprise by any of this. Stick close to the Lord.

SHIFT: Motives matter.

Why are you troubled by the problems with your child? Is it because they could be hurt, or is it because you're hurting? Is it because you care about their spiritual lives, or is it because you are worried about your reputation? This is a good time to be sure that you're operating from pure motives. This is also a good opportunity to confirm your commitment to the Lord. Never allow your children's issues to cause you to abandon your relationship with the Lord. Never.

EDIT: Avoid the blame game.

Check the thought process you're going through, and be careful not to place too much of the blame on yourself. Imperfect parents cannot raise perfect children, period. Also, we need to be careful not to blame it on institutions, such as church, Bible college, or any other place. Ultimately, everyone gets a turn at being hurt in life. The location doesn't do the harm; people do harm. And everyone has to decide how they're going to process the injuries that life deals us.

HANDLE WISELY: Go ahead and grieve.

When a child wanders from the Lord and abandons the principles of Scripture, we may experience a sense of loss. It often takes time to wrap our minds around what has happened and how to proceed. Don't rush this process, and take every concern to the Lord in prayer. Troubles in life make excellent prayer requests. If nothing else, open your Bible to the book of Psalms and begin praying verses from the chapters that apply to your situation. And if you're dealing with something that has you afraid, here is a great verse to memorize:

"What time I am afraid, I will trust in thee." (Psalm 56:3)

FOUR

QUIET STORMS

"He maketh the storm a calm, so that the waves thereof are still." (Psalm 107:29)

QUIET STORMS: THOSE times when things are raging, but no one else can tell. We're still going on with life as usual, but we may be starting and ending our days with the exhaustion that comes from enduring a long, quiet storm. Get a prayer partner and pray together in person or by phone. Don't walk through trials alone. *"A friend loveth at all times, and a brother is born for adversity."* (Proverbs 17:17) I received an email that contained this statement:

"I struggle to keep my spirit sweet under constant negativity."

The wife was referring to how her husband had been stuck in a place of discontentment and pessimism, and her note wasn't the first. There have been many notes and even more conversations over the years where I've heard things like this:

"He hasn't said anything nice to me in years."

"We don't sleep in the same bed anymore."

"He hates his job, so he takes it out on me."

"Ever since our problem with our son/daughter, we've had marriage trouble."

"I found a long list of calls on my husband's cell phone. When I called the number, a woman answered…"

"We are both working full-time, and he works overtime. We still can't pay our bills."

"He is secretly drinking and I don't know how to help him."

"Nothing I do seems to please him."

"My husband doesn't want to go to church anymore."

Problems are like thunderstorms that move in swiftly, bringing strong and often damaging winds. And just like those thunderstorms that are limited to a small area, it may seem like the storm is parked over your house and only your house.

It's hard not to feel a bit resentful when it looks like the sun is shining on everyone else, but remember this: a storm-free life is merely an optical illusion. Everyone has storms. Some have bigger storms than others, but storms don't discriminate.

What causes storms in life? The triggers vary, but here are several more common ones:

- Health problems (physical or mental)

- Job loss or excessive pressure on the job
- Death of a loved one and the grieving that follows
- Repetitive habits from upbringing (men who were reared by an angry parent may have a ferocious temper)
- Despair over failures
- Family issues
- Unresolved conflicts
- Being married a long time

That last "cause" may surprise you, but the longer we're married, the more likely we are to encounter storms. And we're better at hiding problems, because we've had years of practice. Is it right to hide troubles? It depends. If we're keeping things private while seeking solutions, we're exercising discretion.

But if we're just being "great pretenders" so that others won't know that our marriage is on life support, concealing turmoil is not a plan of action; it's a delay of pain.

Can we avoid storms? No, but if it is possible for us to work for peace, that should be our goal. *"If it be possible, as much as lieth in you, live peaceably with all men."* (Romans 12:18)

As suggested in the chapter on "Counsel," ask for the help you need while there is still a marriage left to salvage.

SHIFT: Don't compare.

If we look around at other people's lives, we can easily be led to despair when we're going through quiet storms. It may appear that we're the only ones suffering, when the reality is that everyone suffers in a rotation. Don't look around comparing your life with others. Look to the Lord and lay out your complaints before Him. This is a much better use of energy. *"I poured out my complaint before him; I shewed before him my trouble."* (Psalm 142:2)

EDIT: Revise your perspective.

God often uses circumstances to teach us to view things through His lens of Scripture. We have a default reaction to trials, often considering them to be completely detrimental. Actually, some of our best learning comes through the darkest hours. *"It is good for me that I have been afflicted; that I might learn thy statutes."* (Psalm 119:71)

HANDLE WISELY: Navigate with prayer.

Problems make excellent prayer requests. Scripture is also full of prayer requests that are so appropriate for times of trouble. If you have to cry your way through prayer, pray with tears but pray anyway. Then dry your eyes and tell the Lord that you believe that He is able to deliver you, regardless. Are we only going to love God when things are going well? That would make us "Fair Weather Christians." A famous husband and wife in Scripture suffered one loss on top of the other, each with increasing intensity, and yet when this wife felt like quitting (and many of us don't blame her), her husband Job made an observation and then asked a very pointed question:

> "But he said unto her, Thou speakest as one of the foolish women speaketh. What? shall we receive good at the hand of God, and shall we not receive evil? In all this did not Job sin with his lips." (Job 2:10)

Job and his wife weren't stuck on the rough patch for their entire lives. Scripture tells us that they had double blessings at the end of their traumatic and fiery trials. Eventually, the storm ceased and the clouds broke, allowing the sun to come through.

Sometimes, we may forget what the sun looks like when the clouds have been blocking it for so long. Remember: the sun and the Son are both still there, even during the storm.

Don't give up. It's not over yet, even if it looks really distressing. God will change the situation, change us, or change both.

Trust Him.

"*Thou wilt keep him in perfect peace,
whose mind is stayed on thee:
because he trusteth in thee.*"

(Isaiah 26:3)

FIVE

UNEQUALLY YOKED

"Look not every man on his own things, but every man also on the things of others." (Philippians 2:4)

THE YOUNG WOMAN was strongly cautioned by her parents not to marry the young man that was pursuing her. "He's not the right one," they warned. She wondered how they could possibly know, since they had just met him.

Later, when their marriage hit an extremely rough patch, she said this: "They were right. They could see something I couldn't see, and I wish I had listened."

This admission reminds me of a young man who was driving into an area that had road construction. The signs said "road closed," but he went around them, and not long afterwards, flipped his car on a portion where the road was not paved for driving.

When a Christian marries an unbeliever, that person is headed down a road that was closed by God. It's not surprising that there are multiple car accidents on the very rocky journey into this mismatched married life.

"Be ye not unequally yoked together with unbelievers: for what fellowship hath righteousness with unrighteousness? and what communion hath light with darkness?" (2 Corinthians 6:14)

If you married someone who told you that he was saved, only to later change it to "I don't really believe in God," it's not your fault. You may have even wondered about his spiritual condition during the dating phase, but allowed yourself to be propelled along through the engagement and into marriage without heeding the "warning signs."

He didn't want to go to church, but he would go when you asked.

He never brought a Bible with him, but would glance at yours now and then.

He could sing along to popular songs on the car radio, but wouldn't sing hymns at church.

You saw these signs, but somehow, you talked your way around them, convincing yourself that he would improve after you married him.

You were going to *change* him.

Whether you were warned not to marry your husband or you simply chose to marry an unsaved man, you said "I do," so you are now in a covenant with a person you have promised to love. If things become complicated and difficult, remind yourself that you "signed up for this," and then mentally get a hard hat and some steel-toed boots. You're going to need them for the days when things seem impossibly complicated.

You are not going to change your man, but you can and you must pray for him. Every single day that you live and breathe, pray for your man. Pray from Scripture. Here are some examples of great prayer requests:

1) Lord, please open his eyes to Your Truth. *"Open thou mine eyes, that I may behold wondrous things out of thy law."* (Psalm 119:18)

2) Father, please teach him how to love while you're showing me how to reverence him just as he is. *"Nevertheless let every one of you in particular so love his wife even as himself; and the wife see that she reverence her husband."* (Ephesians 5:33)

3) Dear God, please teach me how to handle these unexpected conflicts wisely. *"He that handleth a matter wisely shall find good: and whoso trusteth in the LORD, happy is he."* (Proverbs 16:20)

4) Lord, please teach me how to live in a way that attracts my husband to You. *"Likewise, ye wives, be in subjection to your own husbands; that, if any obey not the word, they also may without the word be won by the conversation of the wives; While they behold your chaste conversation coupled with fear."* (1 Peter 3:1-2)

SHIFT: Commit.

When you agreed to marry your husband, this made you one flesh. You are no longer two people in God's eyes, so it's time to begin to see yourselves as one in the Lord, even if your husband is unsaved. Stay committed to your marriage covenant.

EDIT: Don't criticize.

No one wants to live with a built-in personal critic. Even if your observation is accurate, criticism is rarely effective and often poorly received.

HANDLE WISELY: Remember to love him.

Do you love your husband, or did you fall in love with the concept of having a wedding and being a bride, only to fall out of love with the realities of being a wife? People can tell when we truly love and cherish them. Can't you tell? If you don't like feeling unloved and unappreciated, turn it around and understand that your husband doesn't like it either. Give him the kind of love you would love to receive, even if it feels one-sided. God loves us fully. We're copying Him.

THERE IS HOPE

"I wait for the LORD, my soul doth wait, and in his word do I hope." (Psalm 130:5)

N O ONE HAS a perfect marriage, because two perfectly imperfect people said "I do." That did it. Your "I do" was a promise, and even in the midst of extremely trying times, your covenant still remains the same. So what can we do with our struggles, battles, conflicts and other rough patches? Keep in mind that the following ideas are limited since this is just a booklet. For more in-depth coverage of these important issues, seek counsel from God's Word and a godly Christian counselor. Until then, here are a few suggestions:

Don't Try Marriage Without God

A person who has a shallow or nonexistent relationship with Christ is needier in his or her relationships with others. The absence of a life with the Lord leaves an emptiness that we may mistakenly try to fill with others. This places undue stress on the people in our lives. We need God, and

we need His Word. Our hearts and minds are more pre-
pared to have healthy interactions when we're women of
the Word. Daily Bible reading is not optional; it's essential.
Salvation is also indispensable. If you are unsure of your
relationship with Christ, settle that before trying to repair
your relationship with your husband. We have no idea how
to be godly wives without God. Our need for a Saviour is
even more evident in our struggles with each other. Christ
has provided us with the ultimate pattern for love. *"But
God commendeth his love toward us, in that, while we were
yet sinners, Christ died for us."* (Romans 5:8) We are all in
need of salvation, so God made it readily available to us:
*"For whosoever shall call upon the name of the Lord shall be
saved."* (Romans 10:13) God teaches us how to truly love
one another from His Word. Sacrificial love does not come
naturally to us.

Respect His Quiet

Life is so stuck in the ON position that people rarely
have time off, regardless of how hard or long they work.
When your husband has a rare period of quiet time, don't
fill it. Even the sound of a single voice may be enough to
disturb the peace. Do you like quiet time? Most people do,
but even if you don't have this need, respect and accept the
fact that your husband may need times of complete blank
space in life.

Tell the Truth

Do you feel like you're drowning in a sea of problems? Does your husband know this? If he doesn't, then choose an appropriate time to have an honest discussion. When we hide how we're feeling, we shouldn't be surprised that our husbands assume that we're handling things just fine.

Sometimes, it may be necessary to have a "Nathan-and- King-David" conversation. In II Samuel 12:4-9, the prophet Nathan painted a word picture of a poor man who had a lamb stolen from his flock by a rich man. When King David heard this story, he was furious and said that the rich man should be put to death and the lamb restored "four-fold," meaning four times as many lambs!

It was easy to want to dole out such harsh punishment until King David was faced with the truth that he was the person being described in illustration. The prophet Nathan nailed King David with these words:

"And Nathan said to David, Thou art the man..." (II Samuel 12:7a)

In other words, "King David, you are the crook I just described."

In a husband and wife situation, it may go something like this:

Wife: "Honey, what would you say to someone who is constantly chewing on people at your job?"

Husband: "I'd probably tell them to consider how they're

making people hate them, and that they need to lighten up and think of the other people for a change."

Wife: "Honey, that's what's happening here at home…"

If you think this approach would open up a healthy discussion, try it. On the other hand, if you're concerned that it would only make things more volatile, hold the words and speak to the Lord instead.

Don't Be Harsh

"We have all this trouble because of YOU!" Now there's a statement that no one wants to hear. Learn to become a wise "editor" and carefully choose words that will build; not tear down. If you're already having rough patches, harsh words will be like sledgehammers to a fragile foundation. Be a wise home-builder. *"Every wise woman buildeth her house: but the foolish plucketh it down with her hands."* (Proverbs 14:1)

Learn to Speak His Language

Your husband has his own unique language. Learn it, and you'll improve your communication. Even the absence of words is a form of communication. For instance, when you ask your husband if he would like to see the pastor for counseling, what does his lengthy pause tell you? If you're not sure, ask him.

In addition to comprehending your husband's language, learn how to speak it fluently. Does your husband want a long, drawn-out novel for an explanation? If not, learn how to speak in shorthand.

Too many words: "We haven't gone on a date in so long I can't even remember when we did, and I'm starting to feel neglected."

Shorthand: "Let's go on a date. Where would you like to go?"

Why say something in 22 words when 11 will do?

And while you're on this date, leave the problems on hold and just enjoy one another for a while. Aim to stay connected with your beloved. Food is often a great "connector," and it also gives you both a time to relax and just delight in time together.

Remember, there is hope. Your marriage has not been forgotten by God, and the Lord is still your Leader and Guide: *"For thou art my rock and my fortress; therefore for thy name's sake lead me, and guide me."* (Psalm 31:3)

We can still "be glad" in the midst of rough patches, because our joy and gladness are not rooted in our husbands; they are anchored in the Lord: *"I will be glad and rejoice in thy mercy: for thou hast considered my trouble; thou hast known my soul in adversities…"* (Psalm 31:7) You don't have to wait to rejoice. You can be glad and rejoice right now.

Rough patches have a way of making us feel cut off

from everyone, but we're never cut off from God: *"For I said in my haste, I am cut off from before thine eyes: nevertheless thou heardest the voice of my supplications when I cried unto thee."* (Psalm 31:22)

God still hears you when you cry out to Him, and He knows what you're going through better than anyone else. Your life is like an unfolding story on a big movie screen before His eyes. Since God already knows all about you, down to the number of hairs on your head, you can take all your concerns about your precious marriage straight to Him in prayer.

Go back in your memory to the good times you've enjoyed as a couple. Surely you can think of more than one good memory? Ask the Lord to restore that kind of joy and contentment to your marriage in the future.

Have you thought of something positive that you admire about your husband? If it's been a while, go there now. Pay him a genuine compliment today, and say "I love you" every day, even if there is no immediate response. When people are hurting, they have a hard time believing that anyone loves them!

Choose a Bible verse to claim as your Anchor, and then hold onto it, reciting it daily and throughout the trials. Pray for reconciliation, repair, or whatever else is needed; but be willing to wait for it. Until then, continue to be a godly woman of hope, knowing that your hope is in and from the

Lord. *"I will lift up mine eyes unto the hills, from whence cometh my help. My help cometh from the* LORD, *which made heaven and earth."* (Psalm 121:1, 2)

Rough patches are temporary, whether they feel like it or not. There truly is hope. What you are going through right now does not define you as a couple, and is not necessarily an indicator of your future happiness together.

Trust God, and walk wisely through your rough patches. Even if things never become what you had envisioned, they may be improved by a shift in perspective, edited responses, and wise handling of situations as they present themselves. God bless you with a wise and understanding heart as you navigate your marital hard spots. He will lead you to smoother ground.

"God be merciful unto us, and bless us;
and cause his face to shine upon us; Selah."
Psalm 67:1

About the Author

FRANCIE TAYLOR IS a wife, mother, and ministry servant. Married to Norman H. Taylor since 1982, the Taylors have three young adult children and one daughter-in-love: Austen and wife Jessica, Hillary, and Collin. In addition to Francie's primary roles in the family, she is also a published author and Editor in Chief at *Keep the Heart*, a publishing ministry for Christian women. Norman and Francie are members of First Baptist Church in Rosemount, Minnesota, where they teach a couples' Sunday school class, as well as serving in various areas of the ministry. Francie also teaches at numerous ladies' conferences and retreats by invitation, covering topics that deal with the "issues of life."

The theme verse for Francie's ministry is Proverbs 4:23: *"Keep thy heart with all diligence; for out of it are the issues of life."* Visit <u>www.keeptheheart.com</u> for additional books, audio lessons, and a digital magazine.

Important Note: This booklet has been written with the Bible as the foundation for the principles noted. To learn more about how a relationship with Christ impacts our lives on this side and beyond, visit this page:

<u>http://www.fbcrosemount.org/salvation/</u>